W9-CGK-928

"Chris Morphew is like Tim Keller for teens. In the *Big Questions* series, he tackles some of today's tough questions with Scripture, wisdom and clarity—and just the right amount of fun to keep young readers turning the page. I cannot wait to put these books into the hands of my three children."

CHAMP THORNTON, Pastor; Author, *The Radical Book for Kids* and *Why Do We Say Good Night?*

"Growing up toward young adulthood can be jarring as we try to figure out who we are and what our place in this world is. In *Who Am I and Why Do I Matter?* Chris Morphew answers those questions in a refreshing, age-appropriate way that is sure to speak to the heart of every young reader. With short, punchy chapters, this book is easy to read and soaked with the gospel. I will be sharing it with each of my own kids and highly recommend it to yours!"

ADAM RAMSEY, Lead Pastor, Liberti Church, Gold Coast, Australia; Network Director for Acts 29 Asia Pacific; Author, *Truth on Fire: Gazing at God until Your Heart Sings*; dad to Alaiya, Benaiah, Ezra, Tayo and Elyana

"Our biggest questions prepare our hearts to hear God's greatest answers. Pick up Chris Morphew's *Big Questions* books and find key gospel responses to your kid's honest questions about God and his plan for sending Jesus."

BARBARA REAOCH, Former Director, Children's Division, Bible Study Fellowship; Author, *A Jesus Christmas* and *A Jesus Easter*

"Passing the faith down to the next generation can seem like a daunting task. Add to that the fact that Christians must also train the next generation to engage skeptics in our faith, and it can seem like an impossibility. This is why I'm thankful for Chris's book, *Who Am I and Why Do I Matter?* He takes one of the core truths of Scripture and explains it in a way that middle-schoolers (and their parents) can understand. I can't wait to put this into my children's hands, and also encourage them to put it into the hands of their unbelieving friends."

JOHN PERRITT, Director of Resources, Reformed Youth Ministries; Author, *Insecure: Fighting Our Lesser Fears with a Greater One*; Host, Local Youth Worker Podcast; father of five

"In *Who am I and Why Do I Matter?* Chris Morphew answers two of the most important questions teenagers are asking today. While he writes in a manner that is accessible to those as young as pre-teens, the content is theologically rich and applicable for students of all ages. The chapters are quick, clear and easy to read. I'm grateful for this book!"

DREW HILL, Author, *Alongside: Loving Teenagers with the Gospel*

"Chris spends his days around young people, and you can tell—his writing is readable, biblical and full of stories. Our young people are being told they can be whoever they want to be. This book tells them who they were created to be. It's a better answer!"

ED DREW, Director, Faith in Kids

WHO AM I AND WHY DO I MATTER?

CHRIS MORPHEW

Illustrated by Emma Randall

To Liam and Alec,
may you never forget who Jesus says you are

Who Am I and Why Do I Matter?
© Chris Morphew 2022. Reprinted 2022.

Published by:
The Good Book Company

thegoodbook.com | thegoodbook.co.uk
thegoodbook.com.au | thegoodbook.co.nz | thegoodbook.co.in

Unless indicated, all Scripture references are taken from the Holy Bible, New International Version. Copyright © 2011 Biblica. Used by permission.

ISBN: 9781784986988 | Printed in the UK

Illustrated by Emma Randall | Design by André Parker

Contents

Chapter 1

SEARCHING FOR THE REAL YOU

A little while back, one of my students at school came to me with a problem.

This girl had moved here from a different school at the beginning of the year, but from what I could tell, she'd settled in really quickly.

She had a bunch of hobbies she really enjoyed and she was already making the most of our school's sport and music and drama programs.

She'd found a fantastic group of friends to hang out with. She had awesome, supportive parents who loved her.

She was fun and enthusiastic and outgoing. On the outside, it seemed like everything was going great for her.

On the inside, it was a different story.

When I asked her what was wrong, it took her a minute to find the words.

"I don't know," she said. "I just—sometimes I just feel like I don't even know who I am. Like, when I'm with one group of friends, I act one way—but then, when I'm with another group of friends, I'm like a completely different person. So how do I know which version of me is the real one?"

"Well," I said slowly, "who are the friends you feel most comfortable around? Where do you most feel like you don't have to act a certain way—like you can just relax and be yourself?"

She listed off the names of a handful of friends and then said, "Yeah, I know I can be myself in front of them, but..."

She trailed off and stared out the window.

After a long moment, she said, "But what if it's all acting? How do I know who the real me even is?"

Sooner or later, I think we all run into questions like this—because unfortunately, figuring out who you really are turns out to be way more complicated than it sounds.

Do you ever look at those people you know who seem to be so effortlessly confident and popular and easy-going—those people who seem like they've got it all figured out—and wonder how they do it? How do they just know the right thing to say and the right way to act in every situation?

Or maybe you *are* one of those people who seem to have it all figured out, and so you know the truth: that it's not as easy as it seems. You might look confident on the outside, but on the inside, you just feel anxious and exhausted—because it turns out that looking effortless takes a lot of effort. You have a feeling that if people knew the truth about your life, they might not be so jealous after all.

ᗑᗕᐧᗑᗕᐧᗑᗕᐧᗑᗕᐧᗑᗕ

Or do you ever feel weighed down by other people's expectations for your life? Does it feel like you can never slow down—like you're constantly working and working to measure up to the standards that other people have set for you? Do you struggle with the nagging feeling that even if you *do* keep working, it still won't be enough—that no matter how hard you try, you might *never* measure up?

Or is it kind of the opposite? Does it feel like no one expects you to ever measure up to *anything*—like they all just think you're a bit annoying and useless? Do you wonder whether it even makes any difference whether you're here or not?

Or maybe it's not *other* people's expectations that are stressing you out. Maybe it's your *own* impossible standards. You have this ideal version of yourself in your head—a version of you who's smarter or more confident or more successful or better looking or all of the above—but no matter how hard you work to become that person, you can never quite seem to get there.

Maybe you wish you could find a way to stop worrying about what everyone else thinks and just be yourself.

Or maybe it's worse than that. Maybe you're worried that *being yourself* is exactly the problem—that if people got one clear look at the *real* you, they'd run the other way.

And look, I know all this might seem like a pretty depressing way to start a book—but the truth is, this stuff is *hard*, right?

We're dropped into this world as helpless little babies and, right from day one, the world is *full* of voices telling us who we are and who we should be.

First, there's our parents and grandparents and other close family. Then, as we get older, there are our teachers, our friends, our definitely-*not*-friends, our coaches, our extended family, and on and on and on. And that's without even mentioning the endless firehose of voices that can come blasting out of our social-media feeds.

Some of those voices are really helpful to pay attention to. Others, not so much. But whether we notice it or not, they all have some kind of impact on how we see ourselves.

So in the middle of all that noise, how do you figure out who the real you is? How do you sort through all those voices and opinions, and figure out the truth about who you are?

What are you supposed to tell yourself when you start to feel like you don't matter, or like you don't measure up, or like the negative voices speaking into your life are *right*? What do you do when you look out at the world around you and wonder where you fit, or if you even fit anywhere at all?

Well, the good news is that you *do* matter. You *do* fit. And the truth about your realest, truest self—the person who God says you are—is better than you can even imagine.

Chapter 2

HOW DO I KNOW I MATTER?

The title of this book is a question—but it's really two questions.

Let's start with the second one: *why do I matter?*

I wonder how that question hits you.

Maybe you have a confident, deep-down feeling that you *do* matter. You might find it hard to explain *why* exactly, but you're sure it's true. You're valuable. You're important. You matter. I mean, that's just *obvious*, right?

Or maybe it isn't. Maybe you're not convinced that you matter at all. Maybe there are people in your life who make you feel like a waste of space. Or maybe that message is coming from the inside—something you just can't seem to stop telling yourself.

But whether or not we *believe* we matter, we all want it to be true, right?

You might not want to be world-famous or to go down in history or whatever, but we all want to feel like we're significant—like it makes a difference that we're here. We want to believe that we matter, and we want other people to believe that we matter too.

And we can go looking for this significance in all kinds of places.

$$\text{⟨}\text{⟩}\text{⟨}\text{⟩}\text{⟨}\text{⟩}\text{⟨}\text{⟩}$$

One popular choice is to look for significance in what you have.

"Of course I matter! Don't you see how rich and successful I am?"

You can focus your life on making money, and then use that money to pay for a big house, a new car, a new phone, expensive clothes, another new car, overseas trips, amazing food, the next new phone...

They say, "Money can't buy happiness". But money can buy you more and more cool stuff and fun experiences and so what if that's basically the same thing?

Plus, money is *impressive*, right? If you've got the newest phone and the latest clothes and the biggest house and the best stuff—if you can throw the best parties and take all your friends to the most amazing places—people are *always* going to want to be around you. They're going to want to *be* you.

And if everyone else is wishing they had your life, you're definitely going to feel like a big deal.

And so even if most of us are never going to reach celebrity billionaire status, it can be so easy to feel like if we had just a *little* bit more money, then we could buy what we needed to make us happy, and to impress the people around us.

Of course, if you're currently living in poverty—if you don't have enough healthy food to eat or clean clothes to wear or a safe home to live in—then, sure, more money will absolutely help you out.

But for the rest of us, I think what we actually need is a change of perspective.

One of the richest people who ever lived was a man named John D. Rockefeller. This guy had way more money than he could ever possibly need. If *anyone* could spend their way to a happy, meaningful life, it was him. But apparently, this one time, a reporter asked him, "How much money is enough?" And do you know what his answer was?

"Just a little bit more."

He was one of the richest people who ever lived, and he *still* thought he didn't have enough. Turns out no matter how much you have, if you're looking to money to make you feel like you matter, you will *always* want just a little bit more.

Because, sure, that new phone is pretty impressive today. But soon enough, your new phone will become your old phone and then you'll need a *new* new phone. Those clothes might be grabbing people's attention today, but just give it a few weeks. Your new clothes will become your old clothes and then you'll want some *new* new clothes.

Which I think is part of why Jesus describes money as a master that, if we're not careful, can turn us into its slaves (Matthew 6 v 24). If you're counting on money to make you feel like you matter, that feeling is always going to be just a little bit out of reach.

You will *always* want just a little bit more.

✕✕✕✕✕

Another popular choice is to look for significance in how you *look*.

"Of course I matter! Don't you see how stunning and popular I am?"

You can focus your life on being beautiful or thin or athletic or fashionable—and then count on that to bring you attention and likes and positive vibes when you look in the mirror.

And if you're thinking, *Wow, that's really shallow, I wouldn't obsess about that*—not so fast.

Because, sure, maybe your life goal isn't to become a social-media influencer—but we still all want to feel comfortable and confident in our own skin, right? And when we *don't* feel that way, it can really mess us around.

Our body image really matters.

But this is *exactly* why finding your value and worth in your appearance is so toxic and dangerous.

For a start, how do you figure out how good you think you look? By comparing yourself to other people, right?

And if you throw in social media, you don't just have the people in your *real* life to compare yourself to. You have the whole internet—countless millions of people to rank yourself against. And when you compare those perfectly posed, edited, filtered pictures to what you see in the mirror first thing in the morning, is it really so surprising that you end up feeling ugly and insecure?

And even if you could somehow change all that—even if you could somehow become the impossibly-perfect version of yourself that you picture in your mind—that still wouldn't take the pressure off. The only change would be that instead of feeling the pressure to *become* beautiful, you'd start feeling the pressure to *stay* beautiful.

Which, in the end, is a battle you can't win—because eventually you'll just get old and wrinkly and lose it all anyway.

If you count on your looks to make you feel like you matter, sooner or later they're going to let you down.

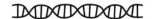

But, ok, maybe you don't need me to tell you not to build your whole life on your money or your looks. Maybe you have some other, more meaningful achievement you want to dedicate your life to.

You might want to represent your country at the Olympics, or open a restaurant, or release an album, or cure a disease, or write a novel, or start a charity.

Great! Those are all fantastic, worthwhile goals.

But if you're counting on any of those things to fill your life with meaning and purpose and happiness—if you're telling yourself, "If I can just achieve *that*, then I'll know that I matter"—get ready to be disappointed.

Why? Well, no matter what your dream or goal or achievement is, there are really only two ways it can go, right?

Either you reach the goal or you don't.

And so let's say you fail. Let's say you *don't* achieve your thing.

Then what?

Well, if that goal was just a goal, you'll work through your disappointment and move on.

But if that achievement was what you were counting on to make you feel important and valuable and worthwhile, then failure isn't just going to be disappointing—it's going to *destroy* you.

If you count on any achievement to prove that you matter, if you make it *that* important to you, and *don't* get it, you'll be miserable.

But in that case, the solution seems simple, right?

Just don't fail.

So let's say you *do* achieve the thing you've been working so hard for. Let's say you win the race, top the class, get the prize.

Congratulations! Well done.

Now you're happy forever, right?

Well, no. You're happy for a while—and that's great.

But no achievement lasts forever. There's always the next race, the next class, the next prize, the next person coming up behind you to break your record.

It's like the money thing all over again. The new achievement quickly becomes the old achievement, and now you need a *new* new achievement.

Which means that if you're counting on your successes or achievements to show the world you matter, you can *never rest.*

You'll just have to keep working and stressing and striving to prove yourself, until eventually you *don't* win—and then you'll be miserable.

The truth is, win or lose, building your identity on your achievements is just another dead end.

But at this point, maybe you think I'm overcomplicating things.

I was talking to a friend of mine about all this recently, and she pointed out what seems to be a pretty simple solution: "Can't we just find a healthy balance of all these things?"

Of *course* obsessing over your money or how you look or your achievements is going to mess you up—so just don't get obsessed. Just enjoy all these things for what they are, do your best to live a good life, and find your meaning and happiness and significance that way.

"Ok. That sounds pretty good," I told my friend, "but how do we actually do it? How do we avoid getting obsessed and find that healthy balance? How do we know what a good life even *is*?"

She shrugged and said, "Yeah. That's the real trick, isn't it?"

So how do we do it? People search for their meaning in all kinds of places—but as we've seen, a lot of those roads are dead ends. So where can we turn to figure it all out?

Well, it seems to me that before you figure out why you matter (or even *if* you matter), you need to figure out who you even *are*.

Chapter 3

WHY CAN'T I just be TRUE TO MYSELF?

If you ask around for advice on how to discover who you really are and how to live your best, most meaningful life, my guess is that you'll hear a whole bunch of stuff like this:

Be true to yourself.

Follow your heart.

Do more of what makes you happy.

In other words, the way to find your true self is by looking *inside* yourself. You need to figure out what you *feel* most deeply and what you want most deeply—and then go chasing after that with everything you've got.

Which seems pretty reasonable on the surface, right?

But dig a little deeper, and it turns out this is not as straightforward as it sounds.

Imagine one of your friends looks deep inside themselves and discovers that what brings them more joy than anything else in the world is setting things on fire. They just love the flicker of the flames, the brilliant orange glow of burning wood, the way the smoke tumbles and swirls up into the sky—not to mention the incredible feeling of *power* they get from burning things down!

Setting things on fire just makes them happy.

And so let's say the next time this friend is over at your place, they decide to light up a match and burn your home to the ground.

"What are you *doing*?" you scream, diving across the room and grabbing their arm a second before the match sets fire to your curtains.

They stare back at you with a puzzled look on their face and say, "What? I was just being true to myself."

My guess is that you're not going to just shrug and drop their arm and say, "Oh, right. Sorry. Go ahead, then."

Because as much as you might want your friend to be happy, you also want to keep having a house to live in.

And, look, obviously that's a pretty ridiculous example. (Or, at least, I hope it is. If not, it may be time to rethink some of the people you're hanging out with.)

But here's my point: the first and most obvious problem with just *being true to yourself* is that there are plenty of situations where doing what makes *you* happy is going to make someone else *unhappy*.

And this isn't just a problem at the burning-someone's-house-down level.

Take a look at your own life. Think about the times when other people have hurt you or betrayed you or let you down—the times when your relationships have been really hard, or when they've fallen apart altogether. How many of those situations have been caused by someone else doing what would make *them* happy without seeming to care very much about how it would make *you* feel?

And on the flip side, how many times have you chased after what you thought would make *you* happy and ended up causing pain and frustration to someone else?

The truth is, if you base your whole life on chasing your own personal happiness, you're going to end up becoming a pretty horrible person.

But, of course, most of us already get that this is a problem. We get that a world full of people just doing what makes *them* happy all the time would be an absolute disaster.

And so, at this point, most people would suggest a slight adjustment: "Do what makes you happy—as long as you don't hurt yourself or someone else".

Which sounds way more reasonable, right?

But let me tell you why I'm still not convinced.

$$\text{DODODODODO}$$

By the time my cousin (who shall remain nameless) was about two years old, he was *sure* he'd figured out what was going to make him happy.

See, he'd been keeping an eye on his mum. He'd seen how, every morning, she would pull the same box from the kitchen cupboard and pour out a bowlful of these tiny pink and brown fish-shaped biscuits. She would set the bowl down in the same corner of the kitchen floor, and then walk away, just leaving them there.

Now, usually, the family cat would come running up and eat all those delicious biscuits—but not today.

Today it was my cousin's turn.

It was time for him to follow his heart—to be true to himself—to do what he knew was going to make him really, truly happy.

And, sure enough, 15 minutes later, my aunt walked back into the kitchen and found her two-year-old son beaming up at her, an empty cat-food dish sitting on his lap.

He was smiling then. But he wasn't smiling for long.

My cousin had been *so* sure that eating an entire bowl of cat food would make him really, truly happy—but an hour later, the ache in his stomach made it all too clear he'd made a terrible mistake.

Now, you might look at that story and say, "Well, obviously *he* didn't know what was going to make him happy. He was two years old! What do you expect?"

And, sure, hopefully we all know better than a two-year-old.

Even by the time I was seven or eight, I could look back on a bunch of the choices I made when I was two and think, "Wow, that was pretty dumb. I'm so glad I know better than that now."

But you know what else is just as true?

By the time I turned 15, I could look back on a bunch of the choices I made when I was eight and think, "Wow, that was pretty dumb. I'm so glad I know better than that now."

And now that I'm an adult, I can look back on a bunch of the choices I made when I was 15 and think, "Wow, that was pretty dumb. I'm so glad I know better than that now."

And that tells me something.

It tells me that even though I like to think I've got it all figured out now—even though I want to believe I'm wise enough to predict what's going to make me happy—I'm probably still wrong half the time.

I bet when I'm 50 I'll look back on a bunch of the choices I'm making today and think, "Wow, that was pretty dumb. I'm so glad I know better than that now."

And I think the same is true for you too.

The problem with *do what makes you happy as long as it doesn't hurt yourself or someone else* is that, honestly, we're just not that good at predicting what's going to hurt ourselves or someone else.

And you don't have to wait until you're 50 to figure this out.

We've all experienced situations where we've tried to help another person, but all we've ended up doing is making things worse. And we've all experienced situations where we've chased after something we were sure would make us happy—but then it didn't.

The world is big and complex and confusing, and we just don't have enough wisdom or information to know for sure that our actions won't end up hurting ourselves or each other.

And that's just when we're honestly trying to do the right thing—which is far from always.

Which brings us to the even deeper problem with being true to ourselves.

The truth is, some of "myself" just isn't all that good or healthy to be true to.

If my deepest desire is to work hard and keep on top of all my school work, then being true to myself is going to work out pretty well for me. But what about all the times when my deepest desire is to lie on the couch and play video games instead?

If my deepest desire is to be kind and generous towards my friends, then being true to myself is going to work out pretty well for the people around me. But what about all the times when my deepest desire is to be selfish or mean?

We might be tempted to look at those negative parts of ourselves and say, "That's not the *real* me"—but who else could it be?

What we really mean is, "That's not who I *want* to be"—and that's great! But this is exactly why just being true to ourselves is way too simplistic.

If we're trying to figure out who we really are, we can't just go chasing after our deepest feelings and wants—because our feelings and wants change all the time, and they contradict each other, and they don't always lead us to healthy places.

We can't just *be true to ourselves*. We need to choose which parts of ourselves to be true to.

We can't just *follow our hearts*. We need to sort through what's *in* our hearts, and figure out what to do with it all.

And to do that, we need someone or something *outside* ourselves. We need some *other* voice that can help us sort through all our thoughts and feelings and figure out who we really are, who we want to be, and how to actually live in a way that matches up with that.

And this is where the people around us come into the picture.

Chapter 4

WHY CAN'T I just listen TO MY FRIENDS?

If you're anything like me, you like to think of yourself as a unique, independent individual. You have your own thoughts and ideas and interests. You form your own opinions. You make your own decisions. You are your own free, independent, one-of-a-kind self.

And that's all true. Sort of.

The thing is, though, as soon as you start trying to *describe* that unique, independent, individual self of yours, you'll realise it's impossible to do that without bringing other people into the picture.

To use myself as an example: who am I?

Well, for starters, I'm a son to my parents. I'm a brother to my sister. I'm an uncle to my niece. I'm a friend to my friends.

These are some of the deepest, most important truths about my identity—and they all involve *other people*.

Ok, sure. But that's not the *whole* story, right? I'm also my own individual self with my own life and career and achievements!

I'm a teacher—of other people.

I write books—for other people to read.

I live in my own apartment—that someone else built.

But, alright, maybe we just haven't gone deep enough yet. Because those things are just what I do, right? They're not who I *am*.

What about all the ways I choose to express myself? Like, what about my clothes? *They're* an expression of my unique personal identity, right?

I dress how I want to dress!

Well, except at work, where I have to wear a shirt and tie to follow my school's dress code.

But on the *weekends*, I dress how I want to dress!

... In clothes made by other people.

... In response to fashion trends that other people made popular.

... So that I can express myself to other people.

Ok. Fine. But that's all just on the outside. What about all my strongest, most deeply-held opinions and values and beliefs? Surely *those* are mine, right?

Well, sure.

Except for the fact that they're all massively influenced by my friends, and by the books I've read, and by the people I follow on social media, and the culture around me.

The truth is, even the deepest, most secret parts of my own heart and mind have been shaped by the people all around me. And even if I hopped on a plane and flew to a desert island, never to speak to another person again, I *still* couldn't escape—because it's already too late. Those other people's voices are already in my head.

And the same is true for you.

It's not that we *aren't* unique individual selves—we absolutely are. But whether we admit it or not, those individual selves are deeply influenced and shaped by the *other* individual selves all around us.

For me, this became crystal clear during my first few years of high school, where I was suddenly surrounded by people who were only too happy to tell me who they thought I was...

The fat kid.

The unpopular kid.

The kid who couldn't play sport.

The kid who didn't fit in.

People say, "It doesn't matter what anyone else thinks of you. What matters is what you think of yourself!"

Which is a nice idea. The only problem is, it's complete garbage.

And if you doubt me, try it. Try having a positive view of yourself when everyone else is telling you you're a waste of space.

The truth is, as much as we might want to deny it, we're created for relationships with other people and we *do* care what they think.

And so what's the solution?

Well, people will tell you to just *ignore the haters and focus on the people who build you up.*

But, again, real life is way more complicated than that.

Because what about the times when people's criticisms of you are *true*? Should you really only listen to people when they tell you what you want to hear?

Or what about the criticisms that feel true inside your own mind, but they're actually way off the mark? How do you filter what's true and what isn't?

What about when the hurtful comments come not from one of *those toxic people out there* but from one of the people we love most?

That bit of advice from a well-meaning friend that leaves you thinking, "Wait—is that really how people see me?"

That passing comment someone made two years ago about how you look that still keeps you up at night.

Those little hints from a teacher or family member that, despite your best efforts, you just don't quite measure up.

How do we deal with all *that*?

Ⅸ⬦Ⅸ⬦Ⅸ⬦Ⅸ⬦Ⅸ⬦Ⅸ

On one hand, we can't live *without* other people's opinions—because if you look inside yourself for your ultimate sense of value and significance, you're just going to wind up in an endless loop of confusion and self-doubt.

But on the other hand, if we *depend* on other people's opinions, it's really going to mess us around. All of us are broken and flawed, and so sooner or later, whether they mean to or not, even our closest people are going to let us down sometimes. So if you look to other people for your ultimate sense of value and significance, you're going to spend the rest of your life riding the rollercoaster of other people's opinions.

And so where does that leave us?

Is there any way to untangle all of this and start moving to a place of health and peace and freedom?

I think there is.

In the New Testament of the Bible, we meet a man named Paul. This guy had no shortage of critics. He'd been mocked, whipped, imprisoned, beaten up, chased out of town, and pelted with stones until he was half-dead. Paul knew what it was like to be on the wrong end of other people's opinions.

But somehow, even after all that, he could still write these words:

> *I care very little if I am judged by you or by any human court; indeed, I do not even judge myself. My conscience is clear, but that does not make me innocent. It is the Lord who judges me. (1 Corinthians 4 v 3-4)*

Paul said he'd found a way to stop being overwhelmed by everyone's opinions (he didn't really care if they judged him) *and* to stop beating himself up about his own failures and weaknesses (he didn't even judge himself).

How did he do it?

It wasn't just by ignoring his haters and being true to himself—he knew that even if his choices *seemed* right to him, that didn't necessarily mean he was innocent.

Paul discovered this freedom by finding another place to turn for love and acceptance and significance—another voice to help him figure out who he was and how he should live.

For Paul, true freedom came from finding his identity in who God said he was.

Chapter 5

HOW CAN I FIND REAL freedom?

L et's take a look back at what we've figured out so far.

We're all searching for meaning and significance in life. We're all trying to work out who we are and where we fit. We all want to know that we matter.

People search for this significance in all kinds of places— in what they own, or how they look, or what they can do— and none of these things are *bad*, exactly. They're just not solid or stable or permanent enough to build our whole lives on. If we trust in any of these things to show us who we are and why we matter, they're going to let us down every single time. We're just going to end up exhausted and disappointed.

So what *won't* let us down?

Well, plenty of people would tell you to trust *yourself*— to look into your heart and let your own deepest feelings guide you. But this is a dead end too, because our deepest feelings change all the time, and they contradict each other, and plenty of them aren't even good or healthy to be true to.

The problem is, as we've just seen, finding our self-worth in other people's approval is just as much of a rollercoaster—and so what we really need is something bigger than ourselves, bigger than people, to lead us and guide us.

Which brings us to God.

Over a thousand years before Paul wrote that letter to the Corinthians about finding his identity in God, his ancient ancestors, the people of Israel, had just escaped from slavery in Egypt. They were camped out at the foot of Mount Sinai, where God was giving them a set of laws to show them how to live as his people.

And the very first law he gave them was this:

> "I am the LORD your God, who brought you out of Egypt, out of the land of slavery. You shall have no other gods before me." (Exodus 20 v 2-3)

Now, part of what God was telling his people here was, *Don't worship Osiris or Isis or Horus or any of the other false gods your slavemasters worshipped back in Egypt. Don't worship Ba'al or Asherah or any of the other false gods they worship in the land where I'm taking you. I am the one true God and you are my people—so worship me.*

But the command went deeper than that.

When God said, "You shall have no other gods before me," he was telling them not to value anyone or anything more than they valued him.

Instead of looking to their money or their stuff or their appearance or their abilities or their friends or their family or *anything else* for their deepest meaning and significance and security in life, God wanted his people to look to *him*.

Which, at first, might seem a bit off-putting.

Was God really *that* lonely and insecure and desperate for attention? Was he really so selfish that he thought everyone should only care about him?

Well, no.

God didn't give his people this rule because he needed anything *from* them, but because he knew it was the best thing *for* them. Sure, God absolutely deserved the love of his people—but he didn't command them to love him because it was something he needed; he did it because it was something *they* needed.

⫘⫘⫘⫘

Generations later, another one of God's people reflected on the laws that God had given them and came to this surprising conclusion:

"I will walk in freedom, for I have devoted myself to your commandments." (Psalm 119 v 45, NLT)

They said they were free because they let God rule and guide their life, and show them the best way to live.

We usually think of freedom as the *opposite* of following rules—but God says that true freedom comes from letting him rule and guide us.

Which, at first, might seem kind of upside down.

But when you think about it, we already get that this is true in plenty of other parts of our lives.

Take sleep, for example. Your body *needs* a decent amount of sleep each night in order to stay healthy.

You can ignore that reality if you want to. You can keep chugging down coffee and energy drinks, keep slapping yourself in the face every time your eyes get heavy—but it's not going to end well for you.

Ignoring your body's need for sleep might feel like freedom in the short term—but eventually, it's going to *destroy* your freedom. It's going to ruin you both physically and mentally, because your body is *designed* to sleep.

Same deal with food. Your body *needs* proper nutrition in order to thrive.

Again, you can ignore that reality if you want to. And living on burgers and fries might feel like freedom at first—but eventually, it's going to ruin you. That kind of diet is going to mess you up, because your body is *designed* for proper nutrition.

If you want lasting health and freedom, you're not going to find it by *ignoring* the things you need to survive.

You're going to find it by embracing reality.

You were designed to thrive on sleep.

You were designed to thrive on real food.

And what God is saying here is that, on an even deeper level, you were designed to thrive on his love and care and guidance.

God is the one who made you—and so figuring out who *he* is and figuring out who *you* are go hand in hand.

The reason trying to invent an identity for ourselves feels so exhausting is that we were never meant to *invent* our identities in the first place.

Your true identity and worth isn't something you need to create or earn or piece together on your own. It's something God *gives* you—something he wants to help you discover as you put him at the centre of your life.

God isn't asking you to throw away your freedom and follow him. He's asking you to follow him so that he can guide you into freedom—into the true life and meaning and purpose that he created you for.

And even though it might sound like God is saying, *Love me more, and love your friends and your family and your life less*, that's not what he's asking you to do at all!

In fact, it's the complete opposite.

God knows that when we put him first—when we let him fill our lives with the love and joy and meaning and purpose we're all searching for—we'll be able to love our friends and family *way* better than we'd ever be able to love them without his help.

And putting God first will also free us to find that "healthy balance" my friend was talking about before—to enjoy our money and our achievements and all the other good gifts God gives us without becoming *obsessed* with them.

As upside down as it might seem at first, when God invites us to make him the most important thing in our lives, he's inviting us on the journey to become our truest, freest selves.

Which brings us to our next question: who *is* our truest, freest self, exactly?

Who does God actually say we are?

Chapter 6

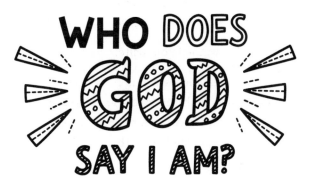

WHO DOES GOD SAY I AM?

Who does God say we are?

What is the purpose of our lives?

What is our deepest, truest identity?

We get a glimpse at the answers on the very first page of the Bible. In these opening paragraphs, God creates the whole universe, fills the earth with a thriving, beautiful ecosystem of plants and animals—and then, last and greatest of all, he creates his masterpiece:

> *So God created mankind in his own image, in the image of God he created them; male and female he created them. (Genesis 1 v 27)*

This verse tells us several really basic—but really important—things about who human beings are.

First, human beings have been created by God.

We're not an accident or a mistake. We're not just random collections of molecules, blindly thrown together by a mindless universe. We've been created on purpose.

Not only that, but we've been created *for* a purpose—which is where this idea that human beings are made "in the image of God" comes in.

The point of an *image* of something is to show you what the original thing looks like—to represent and reflect it.

And so when the Bible says we're made in *God's* image, it's saying we've been created to represent and reflect God in his universe. We've been made to know him, to experience his incredible love and goodness, and then to reflect that love and goodness back to God, and out into the world.

But we're not meant to do it alone.

This is so obvious that you might have skipped right over it, but when God created people, he didn't just create *him* or *her* or *it*.

He created "them".

As in, multiple people.

And so apparently, being God's image is not a one-person job. Apparently, love is *so central* to who God is that the only way we can properly represent and reflect him in the world is *together*, in loving connection with other people.

Which, by the way, also explains what we saw before about how we can't separate our own life out from the lives of other people—we were never meant to! Human life was always meant to be lived in deep, safe, loving community.

Which makes perfect sense when you consider what might be the most mind-bending thing the Bible teaches us about God: his *three-in-oneness*.

The Bible insists that there's only one true God, but that this one God somehow exists in *three* persons: the Father, the Son and the Holy Spirit. These aren't three *different* gods, or three different *bits* of God, or three different *forms* God can take. They're all God, all together, all the time.

How exactly does this work?

I have no idea.

But as weird and confusing as all this might be, it also takes us right to the deepest, most important truth about who God is.

God is not just some lonely old man on a cloud somewhere.

God is a relationship.

God is a community.

God is love.

And so when *we* love one another, we're not just being nice.

We're showing each other the deepest truth about who God is.

We're living out our true purpose in the world.

Human beings have been created by God for perfect, never-ending love and friendship with him—*and* perfect, never-ending love and friendship with each other (Matthew 22:37-40).

And as Genesis continues, we see that the way we're meant to live this out is by ruling the world together:

> *God blessed them and said to them, "Be fruitful and increase in number; fill the earth and subdue it. Rule over the fish in the sea and the birds in the sky and over every living creature that moves on the ground."*
>
> *(Genesis 1 v 28)*

When God says the purpose of our lives is to love him and love others, that doesn't mean we've been created to just sit around feeling warm fuzzy feelings all day.

God wants people to partner with him to fill and rule and explore and take care of his great universe—to work and play and build and create and wonder and invent and discover—to keep filling up on his infinite life and love and goodness, and to reflect that life and love and goodness in everything we do.

God created people for a glorious, eternal destiny and purpose in his great universe—a destiny and purpose that flow right out of God's own vast, unending love for the human race.

And so, obviously, that's all great news for the human race.

But what about for *you*?

See, here's the thing: I love M&Ms. I think they're great. If you have any spare M&Ms, I will gladly take care of them for you.

But that doesn't mean *every* M&M is special to me. If I drop an M&M and it rolls down a drain or whatever, I don't get all miserable about it. I don't call the police and try to get a search party together. I just shrug and think, "Oh well. I have plenty more where that one came from."

And the reason I bring this up is that, when we start talking about God's love, I think this is sometimes how we imagine it.

God tells us over and over again in the Bible that he loves us—but what does that mean, exactly?

Sure, God loves *people*. God says *people* matter. God created *people* for a purpose. But does that mean *every* person matters to him? Does he love each person individually? Or does God love people the way I love M&Ms? Does he just kind of love them as a group?

Because if you see God's love as just this *general* thing, then it can be easy to feel like God doesn't actually love *you* at all. Or that he just kind of loves you by accident—that you just got lumped in with the rest of the group.

You might imagine God sitting up there somewhere saying, "I love everyone!" and then someone points you out and God says, "What? Oh, *that* one? Well, sure, I love them too, I guess. I love everyone."

And if *that's* how you imagine things, then it probably doesn't feel like God actually loves you very much at all.

Thankfully, as Jesus explained, the truth about God's love is something very different:

> *Then Jesus told them this parable: "Suppose one of you has a hundred sheep and loses one of them. Doesn't he leave the ninety-nine in the open country and go after the lost sheep until he finds it? And when he finds it, he joyfully puts it on his shoulders and goes home. Then he calls his friends and neighbours together and says, 'Rejoice with me; I have found my lost sheep.' I tell you that in the same way there will be more rejoicing in heaven over one sinner who repents than over ninety-nine righteous people who do not need to repent." (Luke 15 v 3-7)*

Now, when you read the word shepherd here, don't think *farmer*—because a modern-day farmer doesn't usually have any kind of individual connection with their sheep.

A shepherd back in Jesus' day was different.

A good shepherd *knew* each individual sheep in their flock, and they *cared* for each individual sheep in their flock.

If they lost a sheep, they wouldn't just shrug and think, "Oh well. I have plenty more where that one came from." They'd find it and rescue it.

And when they did, they'd rejoice, because their precious sheep that was lost had been found again!

And Jesus says that *this* is what God's love is like.

God doesn't love you the way I love M&Ms. He doesn't just love us all as one big group. God loves you the way a good shepherd loved his sheep.

God doesn't just say *people* matter.

He says *you* matter.

God doesn't just love *people*.

He loves *you*.

God doesn't just invite *people* into his incredible, glorious purpose and plan for the world.

He invites *you*.

There are plenty of true things about you—your culture, your family background, your abilities and interests and achievements, how you look, how much money you have, who you love and who you can't stand—but what's deeper and truer than *all* of that is that you are made and known and loved by God.

Chapter 7

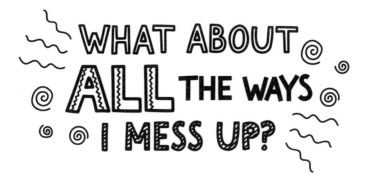

WHAT ABOUT ALL THE WAYS I MESS UP?

Ok. So God has created human beings for lives of perfect love and peace and freedom and friendship with him, and with each other.

That all sounds really great.

Unfortunately, it also sounds almost nothing like the world we actually live in.

If love for God and for one another is the purpose of human life, then, let's face it, the human race is not exactly doing an amazing job of living up to its purpose.

I mean, sure, there are some *incredible* examples of love out there—but the world is also full of war and violence and injustice and heartbreak and every other kind of evil.

If love is the purpose of human life, then something has gone horribly wrong.

And if we're honest with ourselves, we're *all* part of the problem.

The Bible puts it this way: "We all fall short of God's glorious standard" (Romans 3 v 23, NLT).

ⅮⅩⅡⅮⅩⅡⅮⅩⅡⅮⅩⅡ

Picture yourself aiming a bow and arrow at a target. You get the bullseye in your sights, draw back on the bow, and release your arrow. It fires through the air...

And then drops to the ground and lodges itself in the dirt.

You haven't just missed the bullseye.

You've *fallen short* of the target altogether.

And according to the Bible, this is what our lives are like. God has called us to this incredible, glorious purpose— this life of perfect love for God and each other.

That's the target.

The problem is none of us can actually hit it.

Which raises a question: how will God respond, now that we've fallen short of the lives he made us for?

ⅮⅩⅡⅮⅩⅡⅮⅩⅡⅮⅩⅡ

Let's go back to that story Jesus told about the shepherd.

Actually, let's go back just *before* that, to where we meet the two groups of people Jesus told that story to in the first place:

Now the tax collectors and sinners were all gathering round to hear Jesus. But the Pharisees and the teachers of the law muttered, "This man welcomes sinners, and eats with them." (Luke 15 v 1-2)

The tax collectors and sinners were the "bad people"—people who had fallen short of God's glory in big, ugly, obvious ways—people who assumed God *couldn't* love them because they were so bad.

The Pharisees and teachers were the "good people"—at least, they thought so. They kept the rules and, from the outside, looked like they were getting everything right—and so they just assumed God *should* love them because they were so good.

But then Jesus arrived, and he kept hanging out with the tax collectors and sinners—with the "bad people"—and telling them how God loved them and wanted to be their friend. And so, of course, the tax collectors and sinners *loved* Jesus, because for once in their lives, they weren't being told they were too bad for God to love them.

Meanwhile, the Pharisees and teachers saw all this and said, *Whoa. Hang on. If Jesus is a good guy, why is he hanging out with the bad guys? Doesn't he know the only way to get God to accept you is to be really, really good—like us?*

They muttered to each other, "This man welcomes sinners and eats with them".

And *that's* when Jesus told the story about the shepherd.

His point wasn't just to say, *God knows and loves you individually.*

That part is absolutely true. But there's more.

The reason Jesus talked about a shepherd rescuing a lost sheep was to describe what God wants to do for lost *people*—people who have fallen short of God's purpose for their lives and made a mess of their friendship with him.

Jesus *knew* the tax collectors and sinners had messed up. In fact, this was the whole reason he'd come! To find them and rescue them and bring them home—to make a way for them to be friends with God again.

$$\text{\small ▷◁▷◁▷◁▷◁}$$

The Pharisees and teachers were right about one thing.

God had said all along that the *only* way for people to be close to him was by letting him rule and guide their lives—which, as Jesus explained, all came down to perfectly loving God and loving other people (Matthew 22 v 37-40)—and the tax collectors and sinners had obviously fallen short of this.

But the rude shock for the Pharisees and teachers was that Jesus repeatedly pointed out how *they'd* fallen short too. They might have looked really good on the outside, but on the inside, their hearts were just as messed up as anyone else's.

Jesus insisted that the "good people" were every bit as lost as the "bad people". In fact, they were in even *more* danger—because at least the "bad people" were willing to admit they were lost!

Jesus says we *all* fall short of God's glorious standard.

And it's not just that we try our best and still fail. Sure, sometimes we aim at the target and miss—but other times, it's like we're pointing our arrows in the complete opposite direction. We reject God and his purposes altogether because, honestly, we'd rather just do our own thing.

And as a result, Jesus says, we're lost; no matter how hard we might try, we can't get back to God on our own.

Thankfully, we don't need to—because, in Jesus, God has come to us.

$$\bowtie\!\Box\!\bowtie\!\Box\!\bowtie\!\Box\!\bowtie\!\Box\!\bowtie\!\Box$$

Jesus was a human being, made in God's image. But he was so much more than that. He was God himself—God the Son, here on earth as one of us.

Jesus was the one person who perfectly lived out the purpose of a human life—the one person who *didn't* fall short of God's perfect love. But the Pharisees and teachers didn't like hearing that they needed Jesus' help—and so eventually they had Jesus arrested, nailed to a cross, and killed.

But even this was part of God's plan.

Like I said before, the Bible tells us that "we all fall short of God's glorious standard"—but that's only part of the message.

Here's the rest:

> *For everyone has sinned; we all fall short of God's glorious standard. Yet God, in his grace, freely makes us right in his sight. He did this through Christ Jesus when he freed us from the penalty for our sins.*
>
> *(Romans 3 v 23-24, NLT)*

Through his death on the cross, Jesus took the blame for all the ways that we fall short—for all the ways we fail to love the way we should, and for all the evil that this brings into the world. He paid the penalty—took the punishment—that should have been ours.

And then, by coming back to life from the dead, Jesus proved that he really had done everything it took to *freely make us right in God's sight*—to welcome us back home into friendship with God.

Which means that now, if we choose to put our trust in Jesus, we can step back into the abundant, eternal lives we were created for, even though we *don't* hit that target of perfect love—because Jesus has already hit the target for us.

So, when it's all said and done, who are you? Why do you matter? What is the deepest truth about you?

Well, first of all, you are God's precious creation, made in his image for a life of perfect love for God and others. You matter because God says you matter, and there's not a thing in the world anyone else can say to undo that.

However, what's just as true is that you've messed the whole thing up. So have I. So has everyone. We all fall short. We've all done all kinds of wrong to both God and people.

But the story doesn't end there. Not if you choose to accept the rescue Jesus offers you.

If you put your trust in Jesus, you can walk around in the absolute freedom of knowing that Jesus has already taken *all* your sin and shame and failure and brokenness and nailed it to the cross.

You can give up all those other dead-end ways you try to prove that you matter, because you know your deepest, truest identity is a free gift from Jesus: you are a precious, treasured, rescued child of God, and no power in the universe can ever take that away from you.

⨳⨳⨳⨳

What happens in your mind when you hear the words, "God loves you"?

Do you worry that it isn't true? That you've messed up too badly? That God might love *people*, but that he couldn't really love *you*? Has someone made you feel like you're outside the circle of God's love—that you're somehow not included in Jesus' invitation?

They're wrong.

Jesus' death on the cross is the proof that whoever you are and whatever you've done, you are loved and welcomed and included in his invitation.

On the other hand, if you think you don't need Jesus' help—if you're thinking to yourself, *Well, of course God loves me! Who wouldn't?*—then Jesus says you're missing the point too.

Because the other thing the cross shows us about Jesus' love and rescue is that everyone needs it.

Jesus didn't die for you because you're a reasonably good person who just needs a little forgiveness boost to get you over the line. He did it because it was the only way to bring you home to God.

Jesus came and died for you because he loved you so much that not even death was too high a price to pay to welcome you back into his family.

Without Jesus, *everyone* is lost.

But with Jesus, *anyone* can be found.

And the more you trust in God's unfailing love for you— this perfect kindness that sees right through the deepest, darkest, most broken parts of you and *still* calls you precious and loved—the more free you'll be to become who you really are.

Chapter 8

What DIFFERENCE DOES GOD MAKE?

I recently read about this woman who got a new job at a bank. She was excited to hear that she'd be learning how to identify counterfeit money—how to spot the telltale signs that what looked like a real note was actually just a clever fake.

She imagined high-tech equipment and awesome, secret-agent-level training exercises. But when she arrived, her trainer just handed her a stack of real notes and asked her to count them. And recount them. And recount them. Again and again and again.

Why? Because it turns out the best way to recognise counterfeit money is to *really* get to know what real money feels like. The best way to spot the fakes is to be as familiar as possible with the real thing.

And the same thing is true when it comes to figuring out your identity. The more you focus in on your true identity—on who God says you are—the less you'll be knocked off-course by other people's opinions.

We'll come back to that idea in a minute. But first, remember before, when we talked about the idea that God is three-in-one? Take a look at this event from Luke's biography of Jesus, where we catch a glimpse of the relationship between God the Father, God the Son and God the Holy Spirit:

> *When all the people were being baptised, Jesus was baptised too. And as he was praying, heaven was opened and the Holy Spirit descended on him in bodily form like a dove. And a voice came from heaven: "You are my Son, whom I love; with you I am well pleased."*
> *(Luke 3 v 21-22)*

At this point in his life, after spending his first 30 years growing up like pretty much any other person, Jesus was getting ready to step out into three years of public life— three years of travelling around, sharing the good news that, in him, God had come to rescue his people.

Over these next three years, Jesus was going to be *constantly* surrounded by people telling him who he was and who he should be. He was going to be loved and hated and praised and mobbed and misunderstood by accident and misunderstood on purpose. *Everyone* was going to have an opinion about his identity.

But right here, before any of that, God the Father gave Jesus this powerful reminder of who he really was: *You are my precious child. I love you. I am so pleased with you.*

On the very next page, we read these words:

> *Jesus, full of the Holy Spirit, left the Jordan and was led by the Spirit into the wilderness, where for forty days he was tempted by the devil. He ate nothing during those days, and at the end of them he was hungry.*
>
> *(Luke 4 v 1-2)*

Before he went out to begin his public life, Jesus spent almost six weeks in the wilderness without any food. But this wasn't just some weird endurance challenge. Jesus was deliberately taking this time to be alone with his Father, away from all the other voices, focusing and refocusing on the truth about who he was: *You are my precious child. I love you. I am so pleased with you.*

While Jesus was out there in the wilderness, he was confronted by an ancient enemy of God—the one Luke calls "the devil". And the first words we read that came out of this enemy's mouth were, "If you are the Son of God, tell this stone to become bread" (v 3).

If you are the Son of God.

If you are.

This was a direct attack on what God the Father had said

about Jesus' identity: *Are you really who God says you are? Are you sure you can trust him?*

By this point, Jesus would have been hungry and dirty and tired from his stay in the wilderness, and so I always used to read this as God's enemy attacking Jesus at the moment of his greatest weakness.

But recently, I've come to wonder whether I've had it all upside down.

Sure, Jesus was hungry and dirty and tired—but also, what had he been doing this whole time in the desert?

He'd been focusing and refocusing on his true, God-given identity. He'd spent day after day after day with the words of his Father ringing in his ears and sinking down deep into his heart:

You are my precious child. I love you. I am so pleased with you.

And so, when this enemy of God came in and started questioning Jesus' identity, started demanding that Jesus prove himself, started trying to lure Jesus away from his Father—he didn't stand a chance against Jesus.

Why?

Because all the way down to the depths of his soul, *Jesus knew who he was.*

When the enemy tried to derail him with a lie, Jesus fought back with the truth, pulling a quote straight from the Hebrew Bible:

Jesus answered, "It is written: 'Man shall not live on bread alone, but on every word that comes from the mouth of God.'" (Matthew 4 v 4)

Jesus wouldn't be knocked off balance by other people's opinions about who he was. He wouldn't believe the lie that God his Father didn't really love him. He knew it was God, not bread, that truly brings life to people.

It's a bit like that woman with the bank notes. Jesus was so familiar with his realest, truest identity—with who *God* said he was—that when someone came along and tried to lead him off-track with a counterfeit version, Jesus could instantly spot the fake.

And out of this place of deep trust in God his Father, Jesus went on to live a life of peace and joy and confidence and, above all, love for God and others—even in the face of suffering and misunderstanding and rejection.

And now he wants to help you do the same.

▯◁▯◁▯◁▯◁▯

The world is full of voices telling you who you are, and who you should be.

Voices telling you that you don't measure up.

Voices telling you that you need to prove yourself.

Voices telling you that if you just buy this new thing, or have this new experience, or switch to this new opinion, or get the right job, or find the right person, or lose this much weight, or work harder, or do better, maybe *then* it will all make sense, and you can finally be that happy, fulfilled self that the world keeps promising you.

And it's *exhausting*, right?

And, more than that, it's a *lie*.

But the incredible news is that Jesus offers you a better way.

He offers to lead you out of that constant cycle of fear and doubt, and into the life you were made for—to help you reject the counterfeit claims of those other voices and take hold of the real thing.

But it all starts with giving up the doomed project of piecing together your own identity. It starts with turning back to God and accepting the free gift of grace that Jesus died to bring you.

At first, it might seem kind of backwards—finding real freedom by letting someone else guide you—but Jesus insists that it's true:

> *"If you cling to your life, you will lose it; but if you give up your life for me, you will find it."*
>
> *(Matthew 10 v 39, NLT)*

The truth is, on the other side of putting your trust in Jesus, there is *life*.

There's the freedom of knowing that there's nothing

left to do and nothing left to prove—because Jesus has already done it all *for* you.

And there's the freedom of knowing who you really are—that, in Jesus, God says the same thing about you that he says about his own Son:

You are my precious child. I love you. I am so pleased with you.

Chapter 9

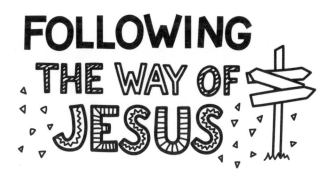

FOLLOWING THE WAY OF JESUS

When you quit trying to create your own identity and start believing the truth God tells you about yourself, at first it might not feel like very much has changed—but the truth is, following Jesus has the power to transform your entire life!

As you put your faith in Jesus—as you trust that he's already hit that target of perfect love for you—God promises to send his Holy Spirit, the same mighty power that brought Jesus back to life, to get to work in your life, helping you to grow into the kind of person who can more fully live out the incredible purpose God created you for (John 14 v 26, Ephesians 1 v 18-20).

This doesn't mean becoming perfect overnight. What it does mean is that, day by day, moment by moment, through all the ups and downs of life, God will transform you to become more like Jesus, filling your life with more and more of the love, joy, peace and freedom that we're all searching for (2 Corinthians 3 v 17-18, Galatians 5 v 22-23).

This change starts the moment you put your trust in Jesus—and it will be completed on the day Jesus returns to heal our broken world and welcome his people into eternal life with him (Philippians 1 v 6, Revelation 21 v 1-5). In the meantime, God promises that nothing in the universe can separate you from his love for you (Romans 8 v 38-39, Ephesians 3 v 16-19).

These are incredible promises—and the death and resurrection of Jesus are the rock-solid proof that they're all absolutely trustworthy and true.

Here's the thing, though: they don't always *feel* true.

Down here in the middle of our ordinary lives, it can sometimes feel like following Jesus doesn't *actually* make any difference at all.

So how do we break out of that feeling? How do we actually *experience* this transformation Jesus promises? How do we live this stuff out in a way that sinks the truth into our hearts and changes our everyday lives?

Imagine an explorer cutting a path through the jungle.

The first time they walk down that path, it's going to be really hard work, hacking all the vines and branches out of the way.

But if they head down the same path the next day, it'll be a bit easier because a bunch of that work is already done.

And the next day, it'll be even easier.

Every trip the explorer takes down that same path is going to be quicker and easier than the one before—until eventually, what used to be a sweaty, exhausting trek becomes as effortless as walking down the street.

And this, scientists have discovered, is also how our brains work.

They call it *neuroplasticity*. The basic idea is that the more your brain repeats a thought pattern, the easier and more natural it becomes for your brain to repeat that same thought pattern the next time.

This explains why our habits are so powerful.

Day by day, repetition by repetition, your habits are literally transforming your mind—which is either good news or bad news, depending on the habit.

The more you compare yourself to other people on social media, the more you become the *kind of person* whose identity is shaped by social media.

On the other hand, the more you look for opportunities to be generous, the more you become the *kind of person* who is naturally generous.

But one way or another, your habits are changing you.

What's the first thing you do when you get up in the morning?

I'm guessing many of you would answer, *Check my phone.*

It's an easy habit to fall into. But it's also a *terrible* way to start your day.

It's not that our phones are all bad—but think about what you're doing the moment you check your notifications or start scrolling through social media. You're hooking yourself into an endless stream of *other people's* opinions and priorities.

Which means that when you start your day on a device, you're giving up your freedom to choose what you're going to head into your day thinking and caring about.

You're letting the internet choose for you.

Or maybe that's not you. Maybe instead of checking your phone when you wake up, you just launch straight into the day—shower, breakfast, throw on your clothes, race out the door.

But whether we start our day with distraction or with busyness, the result is the same: before we even realise it, we're deep into our day without ever giving God a thought.

Which makes me wonder, if God feels distant and only half-real to us, what if that's not because *he* isn't showing up?

What if it's because *we* aren't?

In the Bible, Jesus shows us a very different set of habits:

Very early in the morning, while it was still dark, Jesus got up, left the house and went off to a solitary place, where he prayed. (Mark 1 v 35)

Remember Jesus' 40 days in the wilderness? That wasn't just a one-off thing. The Bible tells us that Jesus *often* went away by himself to a quiet place to pray (Luke 5 v 16)—that he made a regular habit of taking time out to focus his attention on God his Father, to talk to him, and to let *him* set the direction of his day.

Another thing you notice when you read about Jesus in the Bible is how he knew his Bible—what we now call the Old Testament—front to back.

Again, back in the wilderness, when Jesus quoted the Bible to fight back against God's enemy, that wasn't a one-off. All through Jesus' biographies, you see the same pattern repeated over and over again: no matter what situation he found himself in, Jesus always had some wisdom from the Scriptures to guide what he said and did.

"Well, of course *he* could do it," you might say. "Jesus is *God*."

And that's true—but he's also fully human. And in his human life on earth, Jesus got to know the Bible the same way anyone does: by spending lots of time reading or listening to it.

A third habit Jesus committed to was living his life in community.

He made a regular practice of going to the synagogue (where people gathered to worship God). He lived his life in close friendship with his disciples, and he spent so much time hanging out at dinner parties that he got a reputation for being a wild party animal (Matthew 11 v 19).

Remember, reflecting God's image is something God made us to do *together*—and so it makes perfect sense that that's how Jesus did it too.

Pray.

Read the Bible.

Spend time with other followers of Jesus.

Focus your attention on God.

As you can see, none of these are incredible new ideas—but that's exactly the point. We don't need a bunch of new ideas. We just need to live out the old ones—not to *earn* God's love or forgiveness or approval; those things are already ours as a free gift through faith in Jesus.

But as we copy Jesus' habits, God's Spirit will use them to transform our hearts and minds.

So take a moment to think: what might be the next best

step for you to make these habits a more regular part of your life?

⚊⚊⚊⚊⚊⚊⚊⚊

I have to be honest with you: I'm not amazing at any of this.

And I can tell you from experience that when you first start taking this stuff seriously, it's going to feel weird and unnatural and slightly ridiculous—kind of like hacking your way through a jungle.

But I'm learning that the more I repeat these habits, the easier and more life-changing they get.

And so, just as an example, here's what all of this looks like for me.

Each morning (well, ok, *most* mornings), before anything else, before I look at my phone, before I worry about everything I have to do, I try to get up 20 minutes earlier than I strictly speaking have to, grab some breakfast, and for a few moments just... stare out the window.

I pray. I read a bit of the Bible. I pull out a journal and write down a few things I'm grateful for. Basically, as much as possible, before I let all the other voices in, I try to let God set the agenda for my day.

But then of course, the day starts, and I get sucked into the busyness of life, and more often than not, my focus drifts away from God again.

And so the next piece of the puzzle is to just keep asking God, as often as I remember throughout the day, to bring my focus back to him. I ask him to keep reminding me of his love, and to keep showing me the ways he's inviting me to share that love with the people around me.

And of course, God never meant for us to go on this journey alone. We need other people to encourage us and keep us going (Hebrews 10 v 23-25), which is why I also have a church that I go to every Sunday—and friends at that church who I talk and pray and hang out with during the week.

Like I said, I'm no expert.

There's no magic formula here—and, so far, no voices from the clouds or whatever.

Half the time it doesn't feel like anything much is happening at all.

But the more I walk through each day with God, the more I can see God's Spirit transforming me into *the kind of person* who walks through each day with God.

And little by little, I'm learning—not just as an idea but as a real-life experience—that the life Jesus offers us really is the truest, freest, greatest life there is.

Chapter 10

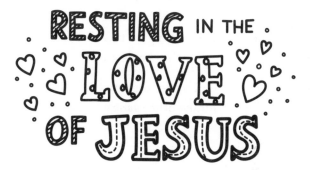

RESTING IN THE LOVE OF JESUS

Before I end this book, there's one more habit from the life of Jesus I want to share with you. I've saved it for last, partly because it's my absolute favourite, but mostly because I've become convinced that the more we practise *this* habit, the better we'll get at practising all the others.

So, what is this incredible activity—this powerful habit that will help you connect more closely with God and your own true identity?

Well, it's pretty simple.

All you have to do is... stop.

⊱•⊰

Remember back at the mountain, when God gave Israel that list of rules to show them how to live as his people?

One of those rules was about something called the Sabbath—a day each week where *everyone* had to stop all their work for a full 24 hours to rest and celebrate and remember God (Deuteronomy 5 v 12-15).

It might seem like a strange thing for God to *command* his people to do—but this rule makes all the sense in the world when you think about who these people were.

Remember, God's people had recently left 400 years of slavery. For centuries, they'd been told that their value and worth were entirely based on what they could *produce* and *achieve* and *do*.

And so one of the reasons God gave his people the Sabbath was as a weekly reminder that they were so much more than this—that their value didn't depend on what they *did*, but on who they *were*: God's precious, rescued, dearly-loved children.

God wanted his people to sit still long enough to remember their true identities. As recovering slaves, it was a message they desperately needed to hear.

And I don't think they're the only ones.

A little while back, I was teaching a bunch of my Year 5 students about these habits from the life of Jesus. We had a fantastic lesson on gratitude. We did a three-week prayer challenge that a bunch of them took up. We had some great chats about Bible reading and community and generous living.

Everything was going fine until we came to the lesson on rest.

As soon as I started talking about the idea of setting aside a day each week to stop and reconnect with God, a weird, uncomfortable silence filled the classroom.

Eventually, a girl put her hand up and said what they were all thinking:

"Mr Morphew, I don't think this one is very realistic. We *can't* take a day off. We don't have time."

⧓⧓⧓⧓⧓⧓

I wonder if you can relate to that feeling.

We live in one of the busiest cultures the world has ever known. Growing up, we're told over and over again that we need to work hard and make the most of every opportunity to succeed in life.

We have so many pressures on us to *keep going*: school and work and sport and hobbies and family commitments and social stuff and jobs that need doing around the house...

And even when we've got nothing on, our phones and other devices often mean we *still* don't stop. There's always a new post to like, a new message to respond to, a new show to catch up on—which means that most of the time, even when we're "resting", we're not really resting. Our lives are still full of noise.

Jesus invites us into a better way of living. Through the Sabbath, he invites us to take regular time out from our endless doing, and to learn to rest in what he's already done *for* us.

(And if you feel like you *can't* take time out to rest, that might just be the biggest clue of all that you desperately need to.)

It might take some negotiating with your family, and some changes to your schedule to make sure you still do all the things you really *need* to do. And, ok, maybe you really *can't* take a whole day off right now. Maybe you can only find an afternoon. Maybe you can only find an hour.

Fine. Great. Start with that.

The key thing here is to take some deliberate, regular time to stop, focus your attention on God, and let him remind you of the truth about who you really are.

Ok. But what do you *do*, exactly?

Well, obviously this habit will look different for everyone, but here's what it looks like for me.

On Saturdays, I do zero work. No getting ready for school the next week. No working on my next book. No ironing or vacuuming or tidying up.

I just stop. Rest. Pray. Read. Go for a walk. I might watch a movie or something, but generally I try not to spend a ton of time on screens. I eat great food. I hang out with my friends and family. I do the stuff that fills me up inside.

And along the way, I slow down long enough to feel all the feelings I haven't had time to feel that week, and think all the thoughts I haven't had time to think.

I let God remind me of everything I've been saying in this book: that even when I stop all my work and all the other ways I try to prove myself, I *still matter*, just because God says I do—that my true value and meaning and purpose and identity are free gifts from God.

And the same is true for you.

⊃⊄⊐⊅⊐⊅⊐⊅⊐⊅⊐⊄

The more you learn to rest in who God says you are, the more that will transform everything else.

You'll be able to enjoy the money and stuff and experiences God sends your way without becoming *obsessed* with any of it—because you know it's all a gift from God, and none of it is even one percent as valuable as the eternal life he's invited you into.

You'll be free to be generous with what you have, knowing that God will always look after you.

You'll be able to celebrate your achievements without becoming self-obsessed—and to celebrate *other people's* achievements just as wholeheartedly as you celebrate your own, because you know life isn't a competition.

And even when you *fail*, that's ok too, because your true identity never came from any of that stuff anyway.

You'll be able to pursue a life of love and peace and generosity and goodness, not as a way of earning or holding onto God's love, but out of the deep freedom and security and peace of knowing you *already have it*.

One of the most vivid memories of my whole life is visiting my niece in hospital on the day she was born.

I remember picking little Hattie up for the very first time, holding this tiny person in my arms, and being just *completely overwhelmed* with love.

I remember thinking, "How is this possible? I just met you! How on earth do I love you *this much* already?"

I'd never felt anything like it before.

And here's the thing: Hattie couldn't *do* anything. Like any newborn, she couldn't even focus her eyes or hold her own head up. When she looked back at me, all she saw was a blur.

Really, Hattie didn't add anything much to the world except dirty nappies and screaming.

But despite all that, I wanted to be with her *all the time*.

I still do.

She doesn't need to do anything.

She doesn't need to prove anything.

She is deeply, completely, unconditionally loved—and she doesn't need to do one single thing to earn it.

And I wonder, what might change in your life if you let it sink down into the core of your being that, in Jesus, that's how God feels about *you*?

What might change if you really let yourself trust that the God who made you has seen you to your darkest depths, and is absolutely committed to you anyway?

What might change if you truly understood that there's *nothing* left to prove?

Could you breathe a little easier?

ⅨⅨⅨⅨ

To finish, let me leave you with this invitation from Jesus:

"Are you tired? Worn out? Burned out on religion? Come to me. Get away with me and you'll recover your life. I'll show you how to take a real rest. Walk with me and work with me—watch how I do it. Learn the unforced rhythms of grace." (Matthew 11 v 28-30, MSG)

My prayer for you as you finish this book is that you would let Jesus teach you the "unforced rhythms of grace"—that you would trust him to show you who you truly are, and to lead you into the abundant life he created you for.

May you come to know, deep in your bones, that you have nothing left to earn or prove or live up to—because life is a gift, and you matter because God says that you matter.

May you live each day with Jesus, and may you find in him the true joy, peace and rest you've been searching for all along.

References

A wise person once told me that creativity is just forgetting who you stole your ideas from—but ironically, I have since forgotten who that person was.

As is the case in all my writing (and, I suspect, almost all writing about these big questions of life and faith), the most helpful and profound ideas in this book are not my own, but were first introduced to me by other people. And so, rather than forgetting who I stole them from, here is my best effort to give credit where credit is due.

Timothy Keller's book, *Counterfeit Gods*, was incredibly helpful to me as I wrote the second chapter of this book. Keller was also the one who first pointed out to me the idea that our future self will *always* be able to look back on our present self and point out a bunch of the ways we weren't as wise as we thought we were.

I first read the observation that social media has dramatically increased the pool of people we have to compare ourselves to in *Ten-Ager* by Madonna King.

The idea that, of all the true things about us, our identity in God is the truest thing, is borrowed from *The Truest Thing About You* by David Lomas.

I read that story about the woman learning to spot counterfeit money in *100 Days to Brave* by Annie F. Downs.

The Ruthless Elimination of Hurry by John Mark Comer is an absolute treasure of a book. Comer was the one who first made clear to me that the wilderness was a place of strength and not weakness for Jesus, and who helped me see the implications of neuroplasticity for our spiritual formation. His teaching on rest was extremely helpful in putting together the final chapter of this book, as was *Beautiful Resistance* by Jon Tyson.

Other helpful books I read while I was preparing to write this one include *The Gift of Being Yourself* by David G. Benner, *Spacemakers* by Daniel Sih, *Making Sense of God* by Timothy Keller, *Adorning the Dark* by Andrew Peterson, *Embodied* by Preston Sprinkle, and *The Rise and Triumph of the Modern Self* by Carl Trueman.

Thank yous

Thanks to Rachel Jones for being such an insightful and patient editor, to André Parker for his awesome cover design, to Emma Randall for the fantastic illustrations, and to the whole team at TGBC for getting behind this series and helping it to be the best it can be.

Huge thanks to Alannah, Fiona, Mirabelle, Sienna, Tyler, Hannah, Micah and Corlette, who read this book first.

Thanks to the staff, students and families of PLC Sydney. It is one of the great privileges of my life to share the good news of Jesus with you every week.

Thanks to Mum and Dad for the countless hours you've poured into talking through my big questions about God over the past 30+ years.

Thanks to Katie and Waz, Phil and Meredith, and Kerryn and Andrew, for your constant love, support, wisdom and encouragement.

Thanks to Hattie, Liam and Alec, for helping me see the love of God more clearly. May you grow up full of big questions, and may you keep turning back to our great King Jesus for the answers.

Thanks to Tom French for being a brilliant writing and podcasting buddy.

Thanks to Rowan McAuley for your friendship and partnership in the gospel, and for being so constantly enthusiastic and encouraging about these books, even though they keep dragging me away from the novels we're meant to be writing.

Last but not least, thanks to my church family at Abbotsford Presbyterian. In particular, a huge shout-out to the whole crew at YCentral—may this book help you to see even more clearly the abundant love God has for you in Jesus.

Keep asking big questions:

△ △△△ △ △△ △△ △

Big Questions is a series of fun and fast-paced books walking you through what the Bible says about some of the big questions of life, helping you to grow in confident and considered faith.

thegoodbook.co.uk/big-questions
thegoodbook.com/big-questions
thegoodbook.com.au/big-questions

Also by Chris Morphew:

A 100-day devotional journey through Mark's fast-paced, action-packed story—bringing you face to face with Jesus: the one who changes everything.

thegoodbook.co.uk/best-news-ever
thegoodbook.com/best-news-ever
thegoodbook.com.au/best-news-ever

the good book
COMPANY

BIBLICAL | RELEVANT | ACCESSIBLE

At The Good Book Company, we are dedicated to helping Christians and local churches grow. We believe that God's growth process always starts with hearing clearly what he has said to us through his timeless word—the Bible.

Ever since we opened our doors in 1991, we have been striving to produce Bible-based resources that bring glory to God. We have grown to become an international provider of user-friendly resources to the Christian community, with believers of all backgrounds and denominations using our books, Bible studies, devotionals, evangelistic resources, and DVD-based courses.

We want to equip ordinary Christians to live for Christ day by day, and churches to grow in their knowledge of God, their love for one another, and the effectiveness of their outreach.

Call us for a discussion of your needs or visit one of our local websites for more information on the resources and services we provide.

Your friends at The Good Book Company

thegoodbook.com | thegoodbook.co.uk
thegoodbook.com.au | thegoodbook.co.nz
thegoodbook.co.in